A View From The Roof

by Dave Carley
based on the stories of Helen Weinzweig

Playwrights Canada Press
Toronto • Canada

A View From The Roof © Copyright 1995 & 1996 David L. Carley
Playwrights Canada Press
54 Wolseley St., 2nd fl. Toronto, Ontario CANADA M5T 1A5
Tel: (416) 703-0201 Fax: (416) 703-0059
e-mail: cdplays@interlog.com   http://www.puc.ca

Based on the stories of Helen Weinzweig from the short story collection
A View From The Roof (Goose Lane Editions - 1989)

Playwrights Canada Press publishes with the generous assistance of
The Canada Council - Writing and Publishing Section
and the Ontario Arts Council.

Cover photo by Vladimir Pavlicik. Cover design by Tony Hamill.
Playwright photo by Michael Lee.

Canadian Cataloguing in Publication Data
Carley, Dave 1955 —
          A view from the roof
A play
ISBN 0-88754- 525-4
I. Title.
PS8555.A7397V53   1997   C812'.54   C97-930300-1
PR9199.3.C37V53   1997

First edition: May 1997.
Printed and bound in Winnipeg, Manitoba, Canada - Kromar Printing Ltd.

For Helen Weinzweig

Dave Carley's plays have been produced across Canada and the United States, and around the world, on stage, radio and television. The award-winning playwright lives in Toronto where he writes, and works as the senior script editor at CBC Radio Performance.

Characters

MISS PERRY
MULGRAVE
HELGA/HANNAH/DAUGHTER
HENRY/DANIEL
MOTHER
BERNIE (can double with MULGRAVE)
BETTY (can double with MISS PERRY)
MAURICIO (can double with HENRY)

Time and Place

The Man Without Memories
Toronto 1975

A View From The Roof
San Juan, 1985

My Mother's Luck
Toronto, 1931

The Bridge of Sighs
Venice, 1938-39

Notes

It is suggested there be an intermission between "My Mother's Luck" and "The Bridge of Sighs".

Style note: Where the last words of a character's speech are bracketed, it is intended that the next speaker override those words.

Production history

A View From The Roof premiered in a Theatre Cognito production at the Tarragon Theatre, June, 1996, with the following cast:

HELGA / HANNAH / DAUGHTER	*Esther Arbeid*
MOTHER	*Kyra Harper*
MULGRAVE / BERNIE	*John Jarvis*
HENRY / DANIEL / MAURICIO	*Alex Poch-Goldin*
MISS PERRY / BETTY	*Gina Wilkinson*

Directed by Michael Waller.
Assistant Director: Chad Dembski.
Production Design: Laurie-Shawn Borzovoy.
Lighting Design: Bob Stamp.
Sound: Steve GordonMarsh.
Costumes: Jocelyn Hublau.
Assistant Designers: Karla Faulconbridge and Mario Moreira.
Stage Manager: Janet Gregor.

Portions of A View From the Roof were produced by CBC Radio Performance (Sandra Rabinovitch - Producer) in 1992 for broadcast on Morningside. Portions were also presented at the Summer Works Festival at the Tarragon Theatre, directed by Michael Waller, featuring Esther Arbeid, D. Garnet Harding, John Jarvis, Maria Vacratsis, and Gina Wilkinson.

A View From The Roof was presented at the Carnegie Mellon Showcase of Plays in Pittsburgh, Pennsylvania, in July 1996, with the following cast:

HENRY / DANIEL / MAURICIO	*Michael Messer*
HELGA / HANNAH / DAUGHTER	*Alison Mould*
MISS PERRY / BETTY	*Mia Backeris*
MULGRAVE / BERNIE	*Randell Haynes*
MOTHER	*Nona Gerard*

Directed by Michael Waller.
Lighting Design: Jyle Nogee.
Sound Design: Alicia Allen.
Stage Manager: Patti Kelly.
Assistant Stage Manager: Garrett McKechnie.
Artistic Director of the Showcase: Frank Gagliano.
Managing Director: Mary Lou Chlipala.

Acknowledgments

Many individuals have assisted in the development of this play and, in particular, the playwright wishes to thank Susanne Alexander, Esther Arbeid, Margaret Carley, Mary Lou Chlipala, Chad Dembski, Frank Gagliano, Janet Gregor, Tony Hamill, D. Garnet Harding, Kyra Harper, John Jarvis, Alex Poch-Goldin, Sandra Rabinovitch, James Roy, Maria Vacratsis, Helen Weinzweig, and Gina Wilkinson. The playwright also wishes to acknowledge, with gratitude, the support of Summer Works Festival, Tarragon Theatre, Carnegie Mellon Showcase of Plays, CBC Radio Performance, George Brown College Theatre School, the Playwrights Union of Canada, the Toronto Arts Council, Ontario Arts Council, and The Canada Council.

Very special thanks to Michael Waller.

Three of the Helen Weinzweig stories comprising *A View From The Roof* are published in the collection of the same name, published by Goose Lane Editions.

The Man Without Memories

1.

*An image: HENRY (DANIEL) at the moment
of escape from the palazzo in "The Bridge of
Sighs"; a young man with a small case or bag,
frozen in flight...*

2.

*Mulgrave Corporation. MISS PERRY, a Jane
Hathawayesque fermenting sexual interior career
secretary, talking furtively on her phone or into
her antiquated headset. She wheels about on an
office chair.*

MISS PERRY   I'm sorry, sir, if I sound, if I sound garbled, if I'm
garbled it's because, well, it's because I'm
nervous. Nervous! And the name Benedict Arnold
springs to mind. Traitor! I'm a traitor phoning
like this but I'm worried. Worried sick sick sick
enough to go behind his back, sick sick but he
needs help. Help! Capital H Help — just a sec.

MISS PERRY checks the door.

OK sorry sorry I thought I heard him. Thought he
was eavesdropping or something well of course
why would he eavesdrop on me he's the boss. And
I'm just — well, this: a Benedict Judas Arnold.
But I've been his secretary for twenty-two years,
that's right, twenty-two, came here in '53, same

year the Queen got crowned. I drowsed through the
Eisenhower years, perked up in Camelot, toked up
in Woodstock... and now it's the 70s, I'm in my
uh uh 40s, I'm staring down into that great
cleavage of despair, stayin' alive in a polyester
disco fever. My point? Sir. I've given this place
the best years of my life and the truth is, I rather
think I've built this company, with Mr.
Mulgrave, oh oh oh now I hear him for sure.

MISS PERRY runs or wheels to door.

He's moving about something's wrong. You
must do something sir. The Board must act,
somehow, please, hurry, I'm a great believer in
privacy; what we do outside of here is our
business I could be a Call Girl. Ha ha, no, no, it's
no time to joke, seriously no jokes, not the right
time, no no. We've always drawn a strict line,
thick line thick thick big thick magic marker line
between office and personal. But now — Mr.
Mulgrave's problems, they're ah — spilling —
gushing — puking all over the corporate
pinstripe.

*MULGRAVE is heard offstage, calling MISS
PERRY.*

Jesus Murphy that's him, must go must go...

*MISS PERRY throws receiver offstage, pulls
steno pad and pencil out of her dress and wheels
over to MULGRAVE area.*

Yes sir yes sir coming sir coming!

MULGRAVE	Miss Perry!
MISS PERRY	Yes sir
MULGRAVE	Miss Perry!
MISS PERRY	Here I am sir.

MULGRAVE   Where were you.

MISS PERRY   Womanly matters.

MULGRAVE   Boyfriends on the phone?

MISS PERRY   A man, yes.

MULGRAVE   *(looking about madly)* Good on you Miss Perry.
                Break his heart. Have a hundred boyfriends, break
                all their hearts. Just not on my time. Where are
                my binoculars?

MISS PERRY   In — on — around — about my desk.

MULGRAVE   Why.

MISS PERRY   Why?

MULGRAVE   Why did you take them!

MISS PERRY   I was — cleaning them for you. I — accidentally
                looked through them last night, noticed a smudge
                (so I—)

MULGRAVE   Don't ever remove them from my office again! Do
                you understand!

MISS PERRY   Yes sir. Yes Mr. Mulgrave, I'll go get them right
                now.

MULGRAVE   They're there.

                *MULGRAVE points; the binoculars are around
                MISS PERRY's neck.*

                You seem flustered.

MISS PERRY   Ex-boyfriend trouble. *(hands over binoculars)*
                Here. Cleaned. Sir have a look, no smudges.

MULGRAVE   Excuse me, Miss Perry. I didn't mean to snap. It's
                just that I'm helpless without them. We're so
                high up and my eyes aren't what they were.

MISS PERRY	Whose eyes are?
MULGRAVE	Not that I'm ancient, but I'm old enough that I can't see down forty stories.
MISS PERRY	*(pointing)* There's smoke!
MULGRAVE	*(fumbling with binoculars)* What!
MISS PERRY	Smoke! From the chimney!
MULGRAVE	*(laughs)* Oh that. Yes, I lit a fire. This morning, before I came in. They arrive after the weekend and I'm worried the house is still a bit damp. And that smell of the wood stove, it's ah yes creating a flood of memories. Miss Perry, after all this planning — they will finally be here, and we can start. The story of my life.

3.

Lights up on HENRY and HELGA standing surrounded by old suitcases. They are wearing ancient, depression-era clothing. HELGA is fakely pregnant. HENRY is mostly in character, and HELGA mostly not.

HENRY	Welcome to our first home, my lovely bride.
HELGA	Oh my God, it really is a time warp.
HENRY	Right down to the skeleton key.
HELGA	So this is the Dirty Thirties.
HENRY	*(trying to cue her to act)* Honey! *(back in character)* I had Farmer uh Jones stop 'round and light a fire for us.
HELGA	I could almost almost believe it's the Thirties, except for the muscle cars out on St. Clair. It's not exactly over-furnished, Henry.

HENRY	For God's sakes, get in character! Yes Helga, I know this is just a humble depression-era farmhouse on the outskirts of Elora and I'm just a poor rock farmer's son — help me —
HELGA	But when you burst into poppa's bakery it was love at first sight.
HENRY	And I know that whatever curves life throws at me, well, so long as I'm with you it will all work out, especially now that your father is taking me into the bakery with him.

HELGA has removed fake baby.

Hey! Keep that on!

HELGA	No!
HENRY	He said to keep it on so he could (remember)
HELGA	Remember. I know. But you don't have to wear this all week. I do. It's awkward. And please, Henry, can we get a deadbolt? You can't see a deadbolt from outside. He'll never know and I'll feel a lot more secure. When Baby Mulgrave arrives, we'll want a deadbolt.
HENRY	No crime in Elora, 1938.
HELGA	How about Toronto, 1975?
HENRY	I'll requisition a deadbolt from Miss Perry. Anything else?
HELGA	A carpet? Baby Mulgrave will want a carpet.

HENRY and HELGA stand for a moment, then burst into laughter.

HENRY	We're crazy!
HELGA	We're insane!

HENRY	Four years of theatre school!
HELGA	We're nuts!
HENRY	No, we're broke!
HELGA	It beats waitering.
HENRY	And he did pick us out of hundreds. Do you know how many actors are jealous of us right now? $1000 a week, indefinite run — just to do improvs?
HELGA	But get a deadbolt, Henry. If we're going to live someone else's life at least I want to be safe.
HENRY	It's top of the list for Miss Perry.
HELGA	Oh my God it just hit me! I'll bet there's no fridge.
HENRY	Not for another six years, not until after the war. Till then: an icebox. The iceman will apparently cometh every other day.
HELGA	Where on earth did Mulgrave find an iceman!
HENRY	I don't know — but he did. Now get pregnant again.
HELGA	Not in here.
HENRY	We can't jeopardize this gig! Helga — please? You're not going to be pregnant forever.
HELGA	Exactly. What happens then? Miss Perry sends a bike courier over and I sign for a baby?
HENRY	A midwife arrives — from somewhere — and you deliver after fifteen very difficult hours. It's in his plot outline.
HELGA	You'll ask for a carpet, too?

HENRY	I'll phone tomorrow. From the library. I'm allowed to go there, if it's research.
HELGA	Meanwhile, I'm confined until Baby Mulgrave is delivered. Confined I might add to one of the two roles allowed women in theatre — whore or earth mother. And I don't even get stuck with the fun one!
HENRY	No, you're stuck in our new old home, an island in a nasty world.
HELGA	More like an island in a nasty parking lot.

4.

Music to indicate the passage of time. MISS PERRY is on the phone again, less furtive.

MISS PERRY	It's getting worse. Sir sir. It kills me to squeal like this, kills me. I'm a Joe Valachi Judas Benedict Arnold — but Jesus Murphy the Board's gotta step in. Now! Before Mulgrave Corp is Mulgrave Toast! It's ah what is it it's three in the afternoon? I am calling with impunity. For all Mr. Mulgrave cares, I could be having a Mazola Roll with the entire 39th Floor. A Mazola Roll. You don't know? Well, you get a bunch of people and you all get au natural and — and then, well, you rub oil all — Mazola oil, no, any supermarket, Never Mind Sir, SIR! My point is: I could be dead! I could be a rotting shell DON'T MISS PERRY ME, MISS PERRY IS NEARING THE END OF HER ROPE! (*stops*) See. He doesn't even hear when I yell. All he does is watch the house and create his autobiography. Helga — his "wife" — is about to have his baby. Meanwhile, Mr. Mulgrave — Henry the actor, that is — goes down to the Central Reference Library to research period items. Every day. Then he phones me. Every day. Then I suggest things to Mr. Mulgrave. "Do you think your family might have had a '32 Philco radio?" I ask. Yes?

Next I spend the rest of the day — your day, your company time, tracking things down while Helga — and what kind of a goddamn stage name does she think that'll make — Helga HELGA — big as a house — she stands on her doorstep, fakely pregnant amidst 160 Mustangs and Firebirds in the Mulgrave Corp parking lot, pretending it's now 1939 rural Ontario and she's about to have Mulgrave's child. All of which is peachy keen, sir — except Mr. Mulgrave never had a wife! He doesn't have a child!

MISS PERRY notices MULGRAVE behind her. She hangs up, throws receiver offstage.

MULGRAVE   Another ex-boyfriend?

MISS PERRY   They won't take yes for an answer.

MULGRAVE   Please — not in office hours.

MISS PERRY   Dinner arrangements only. Was there something?

MULGRAVE   *(remembering)* Miss Perry — can you find me a nursery?

MISS PERRY   You mean, like, a babies-nursery?

MULGRAVE   GARDENING SUPPLIES! I need climbing roses. I just decided — there should be roses on the south north no south wall.

MISS PERRY   Colour?

MULGRAVE   Red. RED! And — and there's a trellis to the side. White. Traditional. Firm, horizontal slats. When I was a child I uh climbed a trellis and fell off. *(holds head down)* See?

MISS PERRY   See what.

MULGRAVE   The scar!

MISS PERRY   There is no scar.

MULGRAVE	I had 16 stitches! That was an awful lot of stitches in those days.
MISS PERRY	Mr. Mulgrave. Sir.
MULGRAVE	Yes?
MISS PERRY	Henry and Helga want to meet with you. They asked if they could come up today, after everyone's gone. Should I clear them with security?
MULGRAVE	*(distracted)* Why — what's wrong?
MISS PERRY	Helga sounded unhappy.
MULGRAVE	Helga's a whiner.
MISS PERRY	Helga's an actor. Shall I go down, and tell them to come up?
MULGRAVE	I suppose. *(raises binoculars)* But wear the proper coat.
MISS PERRY	Pardon?
MULGRAVE	I want you to play the midwife. My child is due soon. The midwife wears a winter coat and has a limp. Can you manage a limp?

MISS PERRY attempts a limp.

Other foot. No, just one foot, I mean the other. Your shoe is built up. Yes, that's perfect. Thank you Miss Perry. You can go fetch them now. I'll be watching.

5.

MULGRAVE's office. All four are present. Throughout the scene MULGRAVE is periodically transfixed by HELGA.

MULGRAVE   It breaks my concentration — to see you here. I
            don't want you here, in 1975. I want you there, in
            1939. It's impossible for me to — create —
            anything when you're standing here, in the
            present, out of character.

HELGA   Well I have the same problem. I mean, I'm OK
            inside that old house but outside it's a parking lot
            full of brand new cars and I'm trying to block
            them out and follow your script guidelines and do
            some intelligent improv — I'm trying to you
            know treat the front stoop like the fourth wall —
            and I can just about do it except for that
            Winnebago parked in front of our parlour window.

MULGRAVE   You whine.

MISS PERRY It's like breathing for her.

MULGRAVE   Hannah never whined.

HELGA   *(under)* Who's Hannah?

MULGRAVE   *(over)* Nevertheless, you have a point. Miss Perry:
            take a memo. Fire whoever owns the Winnebago.

HELGA   Oh well (I didn't mean)

MISS PERRY It's the Vice President's Winnebago!

MULGRAVE   DO AS I SAY! FIRE HIM! Now, was there
            something else?

HENRY   Kind of.

MULGRAVE   "Kind of"?

HENRY   It's kind of I mean sir it's a great job and well—

HELGA   Say it!

HENRY   Well it's kind of (like this)

HELGA   The staring has to stop.

MULGRAVE	Pardon me?
MISS PERRY	*(over)* What!
HENRY	Please sir, (don't be upset)
HELGA	The "staring" stops.
MULGRAVE	The staring is how I remember. The staring is essential. Isn't it, Miss Perry!
MISS PERRY	It's in your contract. Clause 8. The Staring Clause. Right after Clause 7, the Eavesdropping Clause. He does it. And I can do it too. Because I am his Strong Right Arm, his Gimpy Left Leg and Midwife to the Vision.
HELGA	Some aspects of our lives are private.
MISS PERRY	Read your contract Helga Baby.
HENRY	Sir — just the you-know.
MULGRAVE	No I don't know.
HENRY	The man/woman part.
MULGRAVE	Pardon?
HELGA	The sex!
MISS PERRY	You're actors goddamn it! If he wants you to have sex you'll have it and you'll make it goddamn convincing! FAKE IT! *(to HELGA)* You've probably had years of practice.
MULGRAVE	My friends. You have a choice. You can go back there and let me listen and stare. At everything. Or you can pack up and leave.
MISS PERRY	And go be waiters for the next ten years. And slowly become twisted and bitter until you get fired from the restaurant and have to do temp

work. Then before you know it the temp work becomes full time and then—

HELGA   And then all of a sudden you wake up and you're a Miss Perry.

MISS PERRY Why — you — musical-comedy, children's theatre actor!

MULGRAVE   THANK YOU Miss Perry.

MISS PERRY Sorry sir. Sorry.

MULGRAVE   Midwives — never — lose — their — sang-froid.

MISS PERRY Sang-froid. Of course not. Sang-froid restored.

MULGRAVE   Perhaps you could leave us alone for a while.

MISS PERRY Thank you sir.

> *MULGRAVE calms; then turns to HENRY and HELGA as MISS PERRY limps out.*

MULGRAVE   Did I tell you — she's your midwife. You'll be seeing a lot more of her in the next week or two. She has the limp down pat. Now Hannah. I must see what happens — everything, especially what happens next. This is the most important part.

> *HENRY and HELGA still appear to be demurring.*

I'll double your salaries.

HANNAH   *(stops demurring immediately)* I guess if the lighting is tasteful.

HENRY   And the sex scenes are in character.

MULGRAVE   The sex is completely in character! We were always having sex, good sex, joyous sex, all over the palazzo.

HENRY   *(under)* Palazzo?

HELGA   *(under)* What's he on about?

MULGRAVE   *(continuing)* In the library and the great hall and
                 the music room and we were happy, we were
                 really happy, happy as neither of us had ever been
                 or ever would be again but not for long but we
                 were happy and then I — then I — then I —
                 Helga, you look so much like her. When Miss
                 Perry and I went through all the thousands of
                 photographs the actors submitted, the bushels and
                 bushels of them, yours leapt out at me, it just
                 leapt. *(touching her)* Your hair, your eyes, the
                 little notch here where the necklace nestled above
                 your collarbone, I should buy you a necklace I
                 must buy you a necklace...

HELGA   *(under)* Henry?

HENRY   Well, sir. I guess we'll head back now!

HELGA   Turnips are a'boilin!

HENRY   Ice man's a'comin!

HELGA   Baby's a'kickin!

MULGRAVE   Right, yes, there's the door. And on your way
                 out, tell the Midwife to continue holding my
                 calls.

                 6.

                 *Time passes. MISS PERRY is on the phone.
                 She is wearing a 1940s dress and walks with a
                 limp.*

MISS PERRY   Mr. Mulgrave has just ordered everyone on staff to
                 buy a pre-war antique car — or he's firing them!
                 He's showing up in a '32 Bugatti. I don't drive,
                 so I had to buy an old bicycle. Fat wheels. No
                 gears. Hell to pedal. My calves are mammoth. I'm

attracting a completely different kind of man now. Sir: there are entire discos full of men who like nothing more than to chow down on a big, thick, thick juicy bicycle calf. Sorry, sorry. Meanwhile, down on the farm? Helga's rehearsing her birth scene. She's gone into six over-the-top false labours, which I am forced to witness, in my ongoing cameo as the limping midwife. And Mulgrave Corporation is supposed to be sealing that deal in New York. Heck, we're supposed to be *buying* New York! But all Mr. Daniel McDougall Mulgrave does is stand in his office, binoculars in hand, muttering away. Sometimes not even in English! At first I assumed the muttering was Gaelic. But then I distinctly heard him say "bagel". Now I'm no linguist but I have never heard of a bagel roamin' the gloaming. Oh Mr. Chairman — YOU MUST STEP IN MR. CHAIRMAN! YOU MUST SAVE US — NOW!

7.

The farmhouse. HENRY and HELGA. HELGA is giving birth. They are making noises into some kind of intercom.

HELGA

Henry — I think the baby's finally coming!

HENRY

OK honey, hang on, (wait until)

HELGA

No — it's happening now!

HENRY

The midwife phoned — her car is stuck in a snowdrift and the roads are impassible but she says she'll come by dogsled if she has to.

HELGA

More likely she'll come by broomstick.

MISS PERRY bursts in, in her midwife regalia.

MISS PERRY

Damn blizzard nearly got me!

HENRY Oh you made it!

HELGA Praise be!

MISS PERRY Drove into a snowbank outside Guelph. Hitched a buggyride with a Mennonite. Kept warm by singing hymns. Funny things, those Mennonite hymns. Only have one note. *(sings)* "Satan made me shave my beard." How's the water.

HELGA Broke.

MISS PERRY Good. OK Henry — wait outside.

HENRY I want to stay and help.

MISS PERRY Men don't help. Now get lost.

HENRY You don't understand. This is my first-born and I want to be part of the birth experience.

MISS PERRY It's 1939 goddamnit go give someone a cigar!

HELGA It's coming!

MISS PERRY Nonsense! You've got fourteen more hours of labour!

HELGA I'm not doing this for fourteen more hours!

MISS PERRY You'll get overtime! Now BREATHE!

MULGRAVE is becoming visible. He is pacing and muttering. He is clearly upset by what is going on in the farmhouse.

HENRY &
MISS PERRY PUSH!

HELGA pushes and a baby comes out. MISS PERRY immediately wraps it and holds it up for MULGRAVE to see.

MISS PERRY Oh! It's a beautiful little...

HENRY   It's a lovely baby...

HELGA   What is it!

MISS PERRY   Gosh I dunno.

> *They all look at each other. MR. MULGRAVE rushes in.*

MULGRAVE   What is it!

MISS PERRY   *(holds child up)* Sir? Mr. Mulgrave sir? We need a gender.

MULGRAVE   Well I don't know. What I mean is, I only remember the look on her face as I walked out. No, that's a lie. I never looked back. Ersatz memories don't work. My friends, I'm afraid we're going to have to start again.

> *Black.*

A View From The Roof

1.

Caribbean music as lights come up on a hotel balcony. BERNIE is standing, looking out over the city, flossing and brushing. BETTY speaks both directly to BERNIE and MAURICIO (EXT), and to herself (INT).

BERNIE	Hey, look — there's a ship. Come see. Betty? Come see the cruise ship.
BETTY	*(EXT)* Coming dear.
BERNIE	*(pointing)* Can you see it.
BETTY	*(EXT)* Yes dear.

BETTY enters, looking the wrong way.

BERNIE	No, that's the Cathedral. Over there. See the lights strung up.
BETTY	*(EXT)* It's nice Bernie.
BERNIE	Hardly "nice" dear. That's an "If it's Sunday it's Puerto Rico" cruise ship — what a way to see these islands huh?
BETTY	*(EXT)* It's like The Love Boat. And all those rooftops. Little square gardens of cement...
BERNIE	There's the Court House. (The Presidential Palace)

BETTY	*(EXT) (playful)* Let's go out and see the town!
BERNIE	It's too late! You heard Esteves warn us against being out late at night. We should have gone on the bus tour our first day if you'd wanted to see the town.
BETTY	*(EXT)* Aw come on Bernie! Just to the square there and back.
BERNIE	No.
BETTY	*(EXT)* Then I'm going alone.
BERNIE	Professor Esteves especially warned us against letting you ladies go out unescorted.
BETTY	*(EXT)* We're safer here than on Yonge Street!
BERNIE	I'm serious.
BETTY	*(EXT)* So am I.
BERNIE	We're not leaving our room in the middle of the night. This is not Toronto! This is an unpredictable, changeable country. That's why we're here — to study the many irreconcilable elements leading to sporadic outbursts of irrational violence.
BETTY	*(INT with BERNIE)* "Sporadic outbursts of irrational violence".
BERNIE	There are different social pressures here. You don't understand them.
BETTY	*(EXT)* I just wanted to go out.
BERNIE	Well, you can't.
BETTY	*(INT)* It's not a walk I want, Bernie.
BERNIE	By the way, where's the toothpaste.

BETTY	*(EXT)* In the tube.
BERNIE	Don't be like that Betty. Are you tired?
BETTY	*(EXT)* It's been a long day.
BERNIE	Wake you up later?
BETTY	*(EXT)* If you want to.

BERNIE exits.

BERNIE	*(from offstage)* Final reception tomorrow. At the National Gallery.
BETTY	*(INT)* At least there'll be something to look at.

2.

Interval music. Scene is the National Gallery. BETTY and BERNIE are looking at some art, facing the audience.

BERNIE	It's an odd way to see us off.
BETTY	*(EXT)* I rather like it. *(INT)* Beats a banquet.
BERNIE	*(over her last)* Should've been a banquet.
BETTY	*(EXT)* You're so conventional, Bernie! Admire the paintings!
BERNIE	Dear, will you be all right if I leave you for a few minutes? I should speak to Professor Esteves. I'd like to invite him to Toronto.
BETTY	*(EXT)* I'm fine. Go ahead. Shoo.

BERNIE exits; BETTY admires art.

(INT) Alone at last. Bernie schmoozing, everyone praising him. And me, alone at last. And me...

MAURICIO has entered and edged up beside her.

BETTY *(INT)* And a man. And a man standing, beside me.

BETTY looks furtively.

(INT) A man. A man. Standing.

MAURICIO What do you think of it?

BETTY *(EXT)* Me?

MAURICIO I'm curious about your opinion.

BETTY *(EXT)* I uh oh I like his conception it's rather nice the colours all together like that. I'm not a critic. Nice is not an adequate word. *(INT)* Shit! *(EXT)* What do you think?

MAURICIO It's crap.

BETTY *(EXT)* Oh.

MAURICIO It's all a lot of crap. The whole show is a fake.

BETTY *(INT)* I'm not noticing his ethnicity. No no nooo

MAURICIO — It's not art.

BETTY *(INT)* I am unconscious of race.

MAURICIO It's a souvenir.

BETTY *(INT)* It makes me mental to be categorized as Jewish.

MAURICIO It's happy crap.

BETTY *(INT)* So I can't turn around and be aware of his — exotic-ness. Or his youth.

BETTY and MAURICIO move a bit, still looking at paintings.

BETTY	*(EXT)* Do you live here in San Juan?
MAURICIO	Why do you assume that? Could I not be a delegate too?
BETTY	*(INT)* Stupid Betty *(EXT)* I'm sorry I didn't mean to insult you.
MAURICIO	Why should it be an insult to ask if I live in San Juan?
BETTY	*(EXT)* Oh I no I meant — uh I shouldn't jump to conclusions.
MAURICIO	Actually, I don't live too far from your hotel. But I was born and brought up in New York. Like you, I'm an American.
BETTY	*(EXT)* Actually I'm not (American, I'm Canadian)
MAURICIO	I'm an American artist.
BETTY	*(EXT)* You paint!
MAURICIO	I'm an American painter. But I came back. In the States I was made to feel my only value as an artist was because I was Puerto Rican. That's all they saw. That's all they wanted. To give me grants, no, not to me, "Give the Puerto Rican a grant." So I came back. Here — I can finally be an American painter.
BETTY	*(EXT)* It must be terribly frustrating. I don't mean being an American painter, that's lovely *(INT)* "Lovely?" *(EXT)* I mean what do I mean I mean the grant thing, well, it'd be like giving Van Gogh money just because he had partial hearing.
MAURICIO	I knew you would understand.
BETTY	*(INT)* I do? *(EXT)* You did? *(INT)* Ahhh. *(EXT)* Ahhh.

MAURICIO	There are only two genuine works of art in this entire exhibit. The rest are crap.
BETTY	*(EXT)* Which are the — two — good ones?
MAURICIO	Follow me. What is your name?
BETTY	*(EXT)* Oh, it's *(just)* Betty.
MAURICIO	Betty. Betty.
BETTY	*(EXT)* I know I know. Dull. Dull as dishwater. It's not even Elizabeth it's just Betty small b Betty
MAURICIO	*(plays with name)* Bettee. I like your name, Bettee. Follow me, small b Bettee.
	BETTY and MAURICIO move off a bit; BETTY giving only the slightest of glances back in the direction of the departed BERNIE. BETTY and MAURICIO end up facing upstage; their backs are to the audience. The focus becomes now on MAURICIO's hands. BETTY gives her INT by turning to the audience.
BETTY	*(joking, EXT)* How can you say there's only two works of art here!
MAURICIO	I just say it.
BETTY	*(EXT)* But I love these paintings — everyone's so inventive, so — Spanish — no — so — islands — no holds barred; it's cheerful. It's anarchy. I love anarchy! *(INT)* Right, Betty — when it's hung on a wall.
MAURICIO	Here. Look at these. This is art. *(hand lightly on BETTY's back)* These speak the truth.
BETTY	*(EXT)* Yes. They are — nice. *(INT)* I think he's touching me! *(moving her back)* That's his hand. Yes — it's a hand! *(EXT)* Is your work also so — minimalist?

MAURICIO	I can paint in any style. What do you like? Abstract expressionism, realism, hard-edge, op, pop, po-mo, po-po-mo... Anything I do is better than most of the crap here.
BETTY	*(EXT)* Is your work in a gallery?
MAURICIO	I boycott the commercial galleries! They're thieves. I exhibit on my roof.
BETTY	*(EXT, under)* How nice.
MAURICIO	*(over)* If you're really interested — you can visit.
BETTY	*(INT)* Oohh.
MAURICIO	See mine.
BETTY	*(EXT)* I'm only here one more day.
MAURICIO	Visit me tomorrow.
BETTY	*(EXT)* (Oh I uh)
MAURICIO	Here's my card. Mauricio. I'm easy to find. It's a bit of a climb to where I live, but I've marked the way. With crosses. For you. Bettee. Bettee — someone is watching us.
BETTY	*(EXT)* That's Bernie. Thank you for your card.
	MAURICIO has exited. BETTY looks at art. BERNIE arrives.
BERNIE	Professor Esteves has promised to come to Toronto.
BETTY	*(EXT)* That's wonderful Bernie.
BERNIE	Who was that fellow?
BETTY	*(EXT)* What fellow?

BERNIE   The Puerto Rican. He looked like he was talking to you.

BETTY   *(EXT)* No no, he was just standing there.

BERNIE   Probably a gigolo. You know what he'd do, Betty.

BETTY   *(EXT)* What would he do, Bernie?

BERNIE   Charge you fifty bucks US to do what I'd do for free any day of the week. *(laughs)*

BETTY   *(EXT)* He's not a gigolo, he's an artist.

BERNIE   They're all artists, Betty. Everyone's an artist.

BETTY   *(EXT)* Bernie, let's go to the beach tomorrow. I can't go home this pale — I've got to get a hint of a sunburn!

BERNIE   You go. I should draft my reports while they're fresh in my mind. I'll come the day after tomorrow!

BETTY   *(EXT)* That's the day we go home!

BERNIE   Well, you can't have everything. Me go home heap big paleface. Look; we'll come back here someday and live it up; we'll lie on the beach all day, I promise. You go out with the other girls; have a good time; but take the bus!

BERNIE exits, BETTY following. She pulls out MAURICIO's card and looks at it.

3.

Music interlude. BETTY arrives on MAURICIO's roof, puffing.

BETTY   *(EXT)* Mauricio?

MAURICIO has heard her coming and is posing with a brush. He turns with studied artistry.

MAURICIO   Ah — Bettee. You found my studio.

BETTY   *(EXT) (puffing)* I followed the crosses *(suppressed puffing)* It's wonderful up here!

MAURICIO   *(laughing)* Only an American tourist could say that.

BETTY gives an INT glare.

BETTY   *(EXT)* Actually I'm not American (I'm Canadian)

MAURICIO   *(over)* Would you really live in a shack like this, way up on a roof?

BETTY   *(EXT)* I might. *(INT)* Would not. *(EXT)* I might just fool everyone and live on a roof. *(INT)* They'd call me Rooftop Bettee. *(EXT)* Oh, are these yours?

MAURICIO   Do you like them?

BETTY   *(EXT)* Yes.

MAURICIO   Yes?!

BETTY   *(EXT)* Yes. No? Yes. I mean no. Sort of no. *(INT)* Yes? No? *(EXT)* Perhaps they're a bit postcardy?

MAURICIO   Then I didn't paint them.

BETTY   *(EXT)* But they have your name! And your little cross.

MAURICIO   I buy this stuff by the dozen. Others paint them; I just add my signature. My own work — it doesn't sell. It gets good reviews but it doesn't sell. Not to tourists.

BETTY   *(EXT)* I want to see *your* work, Mauricio.

MAURICIO	That is a deeply personal thing.
BETTY	*(EXT)* I would really (love to see them)
MAURICIO	But I know I can trust you, Bettee. OK. These are mine. My Stillborn series. There's three. Concentric circles; each one unmistakably a blind, black embryo.
BETTY	*(groping for words) (EXT)* They're nice. *(INT)* "Nice?" *(EXT)* And, in the middle, your trademark signature — the same black cross. They're nice.
MAURICIO	Nice? This painting — is me. This Stillborn Series — that's my fate, unborn and nameless.
BETTY	*(EXT)* Oh come now! You have a beautiful name and you definitely got yourself born.
MAURICIO	You don't understand — people like you can't.
BETTY	*(EXT)* Try me. Please.
MAURICIO	The agony of the closed circle. You die within it. You never emerge into the full light. You never get born.
BETTY	*(EXT)* But I've never met anyone more alive than you are at this moment! You're young, you're healthy — you're pursuing an exciting career in the arts. Sure, you may not have a house, or a car or anything else — but you have this!
MAURICIO	*(fingering her Star of David pendant)* Easy for you to say. Your husband has a good job. What does he do?
BETTY	He's a psychiatrist.
MAURICIO	See? He has it easy. Where would I have the chance to be a psychiatrist? If I didn't sell lousy pictures to the tourists I'd have to sweep floors and wash dirty dishes. If I didn't sell lousy pictures... Jews have it easy.

BETTY	*(EXT)* Now whoah: just a minute! That's not fair.
MAURICIO	What would a rich American Jew know about not fair.
BETTY	*(EXT)* What would a rich... What do I know about... Well, let's see. I was raised by my grandmother, in two rooms behind her beauty parlour in Toronto, Canada, Mr. Don't Assume Anything. And we were as poor as you are — except we didn't have the benefit of climate. And oh — did I hear you asking where my mother was all this time? My mother — Mr. Tough Life in San Juan — died in the camps. You ever hear of a place called Auschwitz, Mr. Stillborn Concentric Goddamn Circles? You have. Well my mother was grabbed out of Venice, shipped off there, I never knew her. So where's the easy in all that? And God only knows what happened to my father — he disappeared before I was born. Where's the fair in that, Mr. Hard-done By! Oh yeah, my husband the psychiatrist, well he treats me like a doormat, and my kids — if I jumped off that roof I doubt they'd notice until one of them had a birthday and there was no cake so MAYBE I WIN AT HAVING IT NOT EASY! MAYBE I WIN AT UNFAIR! I'm uh sorry. I'm sorry I burst out I don't know what came over me — sorry, sorry — it must be the sun, the sun — it makes one sporadic.
MAURICIO	Don't ever apologize Bettee. You are a woman of passion; I knew that the moment I saw you.
BETTY	*(EXT)* And I really do want to buy a painting. May I see them again?
MAURICIO	The stillborn concentric goddamn circles?
BETTY	Yes. Please.
MAURICIO	Stand back a bit and I'll hold them up for you. *(holding them up)* Number One. Number Two.

BETTY	*(EXT)* That one.
MAURICIO	Stillborn Number Three?
BETTY	*(EXT)* Yes. I like it best. *(INT)* It's a convenient size.
MAURICIO	*(over)* It's a convenient size. $200. I'll give you a bill of sale so you won't have trouble at customs. *(packing)* The moment you spoke to me last night, I knew you are no ordinary woman. You struck me immediately as someone — who has lived, who understands, who was not part of the crowd of psychiatrists.
BETTY	*(EXT)* Actually, they're mostly criminologists.
MAURICIO	Exactly. Head people. But you — you are a heart person, Bettee. You're really very attractive you know.
BETTY	*(EXT)* Do you really think so?
MAURICIO	But you shouldn't cover yourself up with so much clothing. At least let your arms breathe.
BETTY	*(EXT)* My arms — breathe?
MAURICIO	*(over)* You have lovely skin.
BETTY	*(INT)* I do?
MAURICIO	Bettee.
BETTY	*(EXT)* Yes?
MAURICIO	Bettee, I felt right away you are a very sensitive woman who has been hurt, you've closed yourself off, Bettee, shut away your heart—
BETTY	*(EXT)* Yes *(INT)* Yes!
MAURICIO	Come here. Come here. A woman who loves art as you do must unchain her heart...

BETTY	*(INT)* This is it!
	Long kiss; MAURICIO eventually breaks it off gently.
MAURICIO	But, alas, I must leave now. I have to go to my brother's store and let him go home for lunch.
BETTY	*(INT)* This is it?
MAURICIO	If I did not have to help him, we could stay, we could stay and meet the sun together — but then, I think we will meet again, no? Maybe I will come to America again one day, or you will return... Watch your step here.
BETTY	*(INT)* He's leaving, like a shopkeeper closing up.
MAURICIO	Betty — are you coming?
BETTY	*(EXT)* Wait! Just a minute.
MAURICIO	Huh? Bettee?
BETTY	*(holding out bill) (EXT)* Here.
MAURICIO	What's this for?
BETTY	*(EXT, stronger)* Bring us back some lunch. I'm starving. I'm going to stay here a while — get some sun. Is twenty dollars — US — enough?
MAURICIO	Sure. But I'm going to be a long time.
BETTY	*(EXT)* I can wait.
	MAURICIO exits. BETTY stands for a moment, shocked. And then she goes to MAURICIO's paint, picks up a brush, dips and paints while talking.
	(gathers composure) Yes Bernie, the beach is very nice. Yes Bernie, I stuck with the ladies. We encountered no outbursts of irrational violence.

The bus was nice and modern. The tour guide was a bit young. But very instructive. And I learned a lot. The sun is stronger here. You have to be careful. It's so easy — Easy — to miscalculate. You don't feel it at the time. It's only later it hurts.

BETTY stands back to admire her work. She has painted a Star of David over MAURICIO's signature cross.

Black.

My Mother's Luck

SOUND — here and throughout — a restless mix, suggestive of motion, displacement, travel, trains benign and not so benign. Sounds are carefully evocative of 1931. Trickery in sounds. Whistle could be train or steam kettle. Chug of train could be rhythmic chant.

It is 1939. DAUGHTER is standing, holding a suitcase. She remembers her MOTHER from 1931.

DAUGHTER My Mother said. *(sets suitcase down, entering - and staying in - the remembered world of 1931 until the end of the play)*

MOTHER sits painfully down on chair. Long sigh.

MOTHER — I have decided to go with you to New York. To see you off. You sail in four days, who knows if we will ever see each other again.

DAUGHTER My Mother said.

MOTHER No no, stop it. I cannot stand slobbering over me. Anyway, what are you crying for? I thought you wanted to go to your father? I am only trying to do what is best for you. You should be happy, travelling about in style, like a tourist. Not the way we came to this country eh — steerage, like cattle. Hardly what you'd call a pleasure trip. But then, how would I recognise pleasure when I have been working since I was nine?

My feet, my poor feet. I cannot remember when my feet did not hurt. Get me the white basin, the deep one. And pour the water — it should be hot enough now.

> *DAUGHTER will wash and massage MOTHER'S feet for a while, a ritual.*

MOTHER   We will have a talk while I soak. Ah, that feels better already. I am looking foward to sitting on the train. They told me it takes fourteen hours from Toronto to New York. Just think, I will be off my feet a whole day.

Why do you look so miserable? I just do not understand you. First you drive me crazy to go live with your father and now you sit like at a funeral. Tell you what. In New York we will have a little party before your boat sails. We will go to a big fancy restaurant. Me and You and Sam.

DAUGHTER   My Mother said.

MOTHER   Yes. You heard me right. I said: Sam is coming with us.

DAUGHTER   My Mother said.

MOTHER   You might as well know. He is moving in with me next week. Your room. No use leaving it empty. And you do not need to look so worried. I am not marrying him. What for? To give satisfaction to the old yentes, the gossips? Now get a little hot water from the pot.

> *DAUGHTER moves off.*

So tell me, have you got your underwear and stockings clean for the trip? Your shoes need a good polish. You do not need everything new. Let your "rich" father or his fancy new wife from Venice buy you something. I have supported you for sixteen years. That is long enough. God knows as He is my witness I can do no more. And

you remember: It was your idea to get in touch
with your father. Whatever happens you will not
be able to blame me.

DAUGHTER   My Mother said.

DAUGHTER pours new water in pot.

MOTHER   Ah, that is good. Of course, you can come back if
you want. You have a return ticket. You can
thank Sam for that. It was Sam that said a girl
sixteen is old enough to make up her own mind if
she wants to live with her father. You do not
deserve Sam's consideration. The way you treat
him — not talking to him when he greets you on
his Sunday visits.

DAUGHTER   My Mother said.

MOTHER   I know what you say about him to your friends.
And I can still give you a good licking if I have
to. Remember, the smell of sweat is the smell of
honest work. Sam smells a bit; I do not like it
either, but I have had enough from the educated
ones, such as your father, who know everything
except how to raise a sweat. So what is the
difference to me whether they know to take a bath.
Sam will learn. He is a good man, he works hard.
And he has his union to see he gets a decent wage.
What protection has a scholar got? Or me?

DAUGHTER   My Mother said.

MOTHER   I hope you will have it easier than me. Your
father, now he's so rich, can give you the
education your teacher said you should have. There
are good schools in Munich. All I have from life
is sore feet. Look at how calloused and shapeless
they have become. From standing all day. Once I
had such fine hands and feet. So thin. They said I
had the hands and feet of an aristocrat. If you are
really so smart as they say you are, you will not
have to slave like me. Your father tried to educate
me. He taught me to read and write in German.

Oh, I could always tell there was going to be
trouble when he said, "Lily, try and understand..."
Next, a lecture. You would think that after your
father I would not again be trapped by fine words.
But I was. I could never resist a man with a soft
voice and clean fingernails. They would give me
such compliments, they would quote poetry to add
to the feeling. I jump at fine words like a child at
candy. Each time I'd think, this time, it will be
different. But every man was your father all over
again, in a fresh disguise. Sam will be different. A
slight smell is a good sign for me now.

DAUGHTER   My Mother said.

MOTHER   Fetch me the towel. The one I use for the feet, the
torn one. You are sometimes like a stranger around
here, having to be told everything. You can stay up
a little tonight — I feel like talking.

Your father and you will get along, you are both
so clever. Words, he had words for everything. No
matter what the trouble was, he talked his way out
of it. But mouth work alone brings no food to the
table. How was I to know that, young and
inexperienced as I was? When I was married, I was
only a year older than you are now. I was barely
seventeen when your father came home to Poland
on a visit from his university in Zurich. It was
before the war, in 1912. I was only a child when
he fell in love with me. Yet it can hardly be said I
was ever a child. I was put to work at nine, gluing
paper bags. At fourteen I was apprenticed to a
wigmaker. What did I have to look forward to but
more work, more misery and, if I was lucky,
marriage to a butcher's son, with red hands.

DAUGHTER   My Mother said.

MOTHER   So you can imagine when your father began to
court me, how could I resist? He wasn't much to
look at. Short. Pale. Bad teeth. He imagined he
looked like Beethoven. He did. Same high broad
forehead, same angry look. But he had such fine

manners, such an educated way of saying things, such soft hands. He was a man different from anyone I'd ever met. He recited poetry by Goethe and Rilke, he called me "blume" — flower — from a poem that starts, "Du bist wie eine Blume". He did not want a dowry, I would not have to cut my hair. He was a modern man.

DAUGHTER   My Mother said.

MOTHER   So we were married by a rabbi and I went back with him to Switzerland. Four years later, just before you were born, we married again in the city hall in Zurich, so you'd be legal on the records. Let me see, how old is he now? It's 1931, so he must be 47. I bet he never thought he would see his daughter again. He will not be able to deny you — you are the spitting image. Pale like him. Same forehead, those red spots when you get nervous. Even the way you sneaked around, not telling me, writing to Germany until you got his address in Munich.

DAUGHTER   My Mother said.

MOTHER   He was an anarchist. The meetings were in our small room. Every other word was "revolution". Not just the Russian revolution, but art revolution, religious revolution — sex revolution. At first I was frightened by the arguments — until I realized that these intellectuals did not have to do the things they argued about. Where I come from, I was used to real trouble, like sickness and starvations and the pogroms. So I did not pay too much attention until the night we all had a big argument about Nora.

This play, "A Doll's House", shocked everybody. Before you were born, your father sometimes took me to a play. It was a money-waster but I went anyway, because it was nice to sit in a warm theatre, in a soft seat and watch the actors.

That night, we talked to three in the morning about Nora. For the first time I was able to join in. I was the only woman who sympathised with the husband! He gave her everything, treated her like a little doll, loved her like a pet — this is bad? So they have a little argument, she says she must leave him and the children? Leave the children?! Did you ever hear such a thing! The servants know how to run the house better than I do, she tells her husband. Servants! I said to myself — there is your answer. She had it too good!

The men all agreed with me: it was stupid to leave a good life, even a bourgeois one, just to go slave for someone else as a dressmaker. The women — they wore their hair shingled and smoked cigarettes and beside them I felt like a sack of potatoes — the women were disappointed in their comrades — could these revolutionaries not see Nora was being exploited by her husband? And back and forth like this, the rest of the night.

But the next day, I could still think of nothing but what Nora did. It never occurred to me that a woman leaves a man except if he beats her. But it made sense.

From that time on, I began to change. I shingled my hair, I sat in the cafes and smoked. When I got pregnant I refused to go for an abortion like your father wanted, and you were born. Your father had to leave university and be a clerk in a shoe store. He hated the job, he hated me. You cried a lot. Nothing in your father's books explained why you cried so much. Then he talked me into going back to work; they were glad to have me back at the beauty parlour. Your father was glad to get back to his books.

DAUGHTER   My Mother said.

MOTHER   One day, winter, I came back from work to our cold room and dirty sheets, and our six dishes and our two pots sticky with food. There was not a

penny for the gas and I could not heat your milk.
You cried, your father yelled he could not study.
After going to university for four years, I could
not understand why he needed still to study. I had
to get up six in the morning to take you to the
creche at one end of the city, and go to work at the
other end. You would not stop screaming and I
spanked you. Your father said I was stupid to take
out my bad feelings on an innocent child. I sat
down, beaten.

In that moment I knew I was going to leave.
There is a second, no longer than the blink of an
eye, when husband and wife turn into strangers.
They could pass in the street and not know each
other. That's what happened that night.

DAUGHTER   My Mother said.

MOTHER   Two days later, I left our room with you. We took
the train to Hamburg. I had managed to save a bit,
my tip money. I bought underwear for us, a new
sweater for me and a nice little red coat for you.
We took the boat to New York. A sailor gave you
a navy blue sailor hat with the name of the boat,
"George Washington", in gold on a ribbon around
it. You wore it day and night, on Ellis Island, on
the train to Toronto.

Travel, train montage rises under.

One o'clock already! We should be in our beds!
First, wash the cups. Hannah; you know I cannot
stand mess in the kitchen. Remember, never leave
dirty dishes around. Show your father I brought
you up right. Which reminds me, did you buy
rolls like I told you? Good. Sam likes a fresh roll
with lox for Sunday. Just think, in a week you
will be on the ocean and not so long after that,
Germany.

DAUGHTER   My Mother said...

MOTHER   Go already. I will turn out the light.

DAUGHTER   My Mother said...

MOTHER   Go! Go my little flower! Go!

> *Travel sound comes up over MOTHER; ends in threatening burst. DAUGHTER returns to 1939, picks up suitcase, and takes a few steps back.*
>
> *Black.*

The Bridge of Sighs

1.

An image, a split-second one of DANIEL, frozen at the moment of his eventual leaving of HANNAH in Venice. There are two stages to the pose — a hearing image and a leaving image. The image is an exact repeat of the scene that began "The Man Without Memories" and the image that occurs later in "The Bridge of Sighs", during his actual flight from Venice.

2.

A town in Austria. Mid-November, 1938. The Kanzler family bakery. As the lights come up, HANNAH is pacing, looking anxiously outside at her car. Music builds then out.

ISAAC (*offstage voice, shouting*) Go! Go my son! GO!

DANIEL is pushed out of the back of shop. He is holding a coat and a bag of baked goods. He skids to a stop in front of HANNAH. She holds up keys for him. Both HANNAH and DANIEL are frightened, to varying degrees.

DANIEL I don't want to leave him!

HANNAH Get in the car!

DANIEL Get someone else!

HANNAH	DRIVE!
DANIEL	NO!
HANNAH	Drive.

3.

Minutes later. Driving out of town and into country. DANIEL is concentrating with great intensity.

HANNAH   Your father is a fast thinker. It took him all of two minutes to understand you should go. You on the other hand you require a conference to make up your mind.

DANIEL   You think you can just barge into (the shop and)

HANNAH   Keep your eyes on the road. And don't think you're doing me any favours. I'd have preferred your brother. I didn't even know you existed. Every time we stopped at the bakery you were what — playing marbles? Why is the car roaring — shouldn't you be in another gear?

DANIEL   I don't know.

HANNAH   *(poking him)* Try another gear, Squirt.

DANIEL   I could drive better (if you'd stop poking me)

HANNAH   There, see? That's better. Bet you never thought you'd be driving a Bugatti.

DANIEL   I'm driving you across the border then I'm coming back.

HANNAH   You'll drive me as far as I tell you. Now pull over.

4 .

> *Side of the road. DANIEL is out of the car.*
> *Sound of countryside.*

HANNAH   Take your pants off. NOW! Hurry up! No, don't
bother folding your shirt — throw it behind that
hedge. Your pants too. Snap to it — we don't
have a lot of time. They could be following us.
Hey Squirt — you're bigger than I thought.

DANIEL   Stop calling me Squirt.

HANNAH   You have a better name?

DANIEL   Daniel.

HANNAH   Well — OK — you're not your brother but you
have gotten us ten miles without mishap, fair's
fair: Daniel.

> *DANIEL is stripped to his undies and is*
> *standing there shyly.*

DANIEL   I'm freezing.

> *HANNAH hands him clothes.*

HANNAH   Here. It was our chauffeur's spare set. We insisted
he wear clean uniforms. It wasn't something he
did naturally — changing clothes — he was a
peasant, a real stinker. Between April and October
(groans). Now, November comes, he's finally
bearable — and he turns into a coward when it
comes to crossing borders. What was he doing
back there — running off... Thankfully I
remembered your father's bakery.

> *DANIEL is now dressed in chauffeur's clothes;*
> *they are a few sizes too big. HANNAH giggles.*

DANIEL   What was his name — Goliath?

HANNAH   You'll grow into them by Venice.

5.

Driving. HANNAH is eating DANIEL's baked goods — perhaps passing him some after testing, or he may be trying to get them back from her.

HANNAH	You're a quick learner.
DANIEL	It's a beautiful car. Miss, why didn't you take the train across?
HANNAH	Everyone's taking the train. Trains get stopped.
DANIEL	So do cars.
HANNAH	Yes but you can park cars, and walk. Not that I would. Walk. You'd have to be part mountain goat here. Plus it would be a waste of a Bugatti. These are good tägelach.
DANIEL	Rögeluch.
HANNAH	Tägelach rögeluch.
DANIEL	They're rögeluch. I should know. And they're not just "good", they're the best in Austria. But Miss, this car — it draws attention — everyone we drive by stares (at us)
HANNAH	It inspires respect. People inch up to Bugattis, like they're approaching royalty. They'll gawk, but they won't touch. Not immediately. The same thing happens with our Isotta.
DANIEL	You have an Isotta!
HANNAH	Careful! Yes.
DANIEL	Why didn't you bring it!
HANNAH	Suddenly a Bugatti's not good enough? Isottas are unreliable. They break down.

Sound of gear grinding.

DANIEL   Damn!

HANNAH   I imagine your big brother would shift gears smoothly.

DANIEL   Don't talk about my brother.

HANNAH   He was very famous, your brother. As far north as Munich even, women would say, stop at Kanzler's Bakery in Steinach — the best — whatever — in Austria — *(holds one up)* it's true — and an enormous young man behind the counter. Your brother must've had dozens of girlfriends.

DANIEL   I had one too.

HANNAH   A girlfriend? No.

DANIEL   Yes.

HANNAH   You're too young. OK, what was her name?

DANIEL   Never mind.

HANNAH   What was her name!

DANIEL   That's private information.

HANNAH   I bet I know. One of the Palm Sisters. But which one — Miss Left Palm or Miss Right?

DANIEL   You have a dirty mouth. Owning a Bugatti doesn't give you the right to be filthy. I promised my father I'd drive you but I never promised to listen to gutter talk (you should be ashamed)

HANNAH   How old are you? 18? I was a prude too, when I was 18. What a difference six years make. We should find a farmer's lane or somewhere, to spend the night.

6.

They have pulled over in a farmer's lane. Night.

HANNAH   We'll time it so we get there at noon. When it's busiest and they're thinking only about lunch.

DANIEL   Who's "they"?

HANNAH   Guess. There's no problem actually getting *into* Italy — our challenge is getting *out of* Austria. The Nazis are checking everyone leaving — mostly to make sure we're not hauling out treasures.

DANIEL   Are you?

HANNAH   Don't worry. I've got this necklace, that's all.

DANIEL   We heard that they were detaining (people)

HANNAH   They are, but we have some advantages. The car instills respect and I can act like the Queen of Sheba.

DANIEL   *(muttering under)* No surprise.

HANNAH   You'd be well off to act arrogant too. A Bugatti chauffeur is several notches above a border guard. Come on Sq — Daniel — give me haughty.

        DANIEL tries; HANNAH laughs. This is a little bit of fun for DANIEL, as well.

That's a toothache. You're chauffeuring the daughter of one of the richest men in Munich, a famous professor. That's better. *(pokes him)*

        DANIEL does a better haughty.

Perfect! Finally, there's the matter of passports. Mine's Canadian. If I was German it would now have a capital J on it and they'd really tear the car apart. You can use my driver's. It's in the glove compartment. Memorize the details. But let me do the talking.

7.

Later that night. DANIEL is standing beside HANNAH; watching her sleep. He reaches out and touches her hair, then her necklace. She stirs. He pulls back. He leans down and smells her hair. She stirs. He pulls back and she wakens.

HANNAH	What are you doing.
DANIEL	Standing guard.
HANNAH	When I told you to keep watch, I didn't mean watch me.
DANIEL	*(touching the necklace)* Are you really going to pay me with that?
HANNAH	This?
DANIEL	You promised my father. Is it real?
HANNAH	Every stone. But what would you want with a necklace?
DANIEL	I'll buy a passage somewhere.
HANNAH	Somewhere where.
DANIEL	America. Canada.
HANNAH	Canada won't take you.
DANIEL	Why not?
HANNAH	Capital J.
DANIEL	But aren't you going there?

HANNAH	Absolutely not.
DANIEL	Your passport is Canadian — you must have (some connection)
HANNAH	I'm only going as far as Venice. My stepmother's home is there, it's a civilized city. It'll be the perfect place to — live with my father.
DANIEL	My brother always wanted to go to Argentina. He said that was the perfect place.
HANNAH	Where was your brother? Why wasn't he behind the counter like always?
DANIEL	He was arrested. Three days ago, in Innsbruck.
HANNAH	Were there charges?
DANIEL	They said he was a Communist.
HANNAH	Was he?
DANIEL	Yes. He was at a meeting, there was a raid. One of his friends escaped and got word to us. Father and I cleaned out his room, looking for — anything, anything that might get him, us, in trouble, and we found leaflets.
HANNAH	I hope you burned them.
DANIEL	Better than that! Father's been requisitioned to make bread for the local garrison, for the Nazis, so we shredded the leaflets — and baked them into loaves. It gave the bread a lumpen grey texture — they loved it.
HANNAH	*(laughs)* Your father has a sense of humour. He'll need it. And at least you know where he is. My parents were called to Berlin at the end of last month, to attend some sort of forum. Nothing unusual. But two weeks passed, no letters, no telegrams...

DANIEL   That doesn't mean (that they're)

HANNAH   Oh I know. Father's very negligent and my
          mother — stepmother — becomes distracted in
          cities with stores.

DANIEL   Then (perhaps it's just)

HANNAH   Except, a telegram came yesterday, from my
          father, through a colleague, ordering me to go to
          our home in Venice. I can only assume he's been
          detained somewhere.

DANIEL   But he's famous!

HANNAH   Yes and whatever's happened will be temporary,
          he has colleagues all over the world, they can
          speak up on his behalf.

DANIEL   My father's just a baker.

HANNAH   Bakers are more useful than professors. The
          garrison will need its lumpen bread. Two weeks
          ago I still believed this would pass. But now, after
          what I saw in Munich last week, stores burned,
          respectable, educated citizens beaten just for
          walking down a street, then the telegram...

DANIEL   Are you worried about tomorrow?

HANNAH   *(recovering)* No. I've got the car and the passport
          and — yes. Yes I am scared, a little. But Daniel
          — you can go back to your father. I can give you
          some money for food. I won't have it on my
          conscience that you didn't have a choice.

DANIEL   My father won't leave Austria until he knows
          about my brother.

          Pause.

HANNAH   Please Daniel. Take me across.

          Pause.

DANIEL	Both our fathers were saying the same thing.
HANNAH	"Go."
DANIEL	"Go."

8.

The border. Sound to indicate a military presence.

HANNAH

(as Guard approaches, to DANIEL) Here he comes. Follow my lead. Just let me talk. *(to GUARD, haughtily, but nervous)* Good afternoon. *(holds out passport disdainfully; internal)* Mouthbreather. Peasant. Hayseed. *(EXT)* It's Canadian. *(INT)* Oaf. Thug. Nazi. *(EXT)* I realize it says 'Birthplace: Switzerland' but my nationality is Canadian, I've been a Canadian since I was two it says so right there. *(INT)* Oh God let me through. Peasant.

She gets passport back and watches as GUARD walks around to DANIEL.

DANIEL

Good afternoon. *(holds out passport, prays internally)* God if you let me across, if you do this for me, I will live a life of purity and I will study and I will lust after no woman but my eventual wife. And I will never ever masturbate on the Sabbath — or any other day — and I will always observe — *(EXT)* Get out? *(gets out of car, gets a brainwave, speaks to guard)* Nice car, isn't it! It's a Type 49! They only made 500. 8 cylinders, maximum speed 145. This particular model was designed by Ettore Bugatti himself. The Great Bugatti! And they said the French couldn't build cars! *(quickly)* Of course it's no Mercedes, if I had my choice I'd be driving a Mercedes. Madam also owns an Isotta but Isottas are too unreliable for holiday travel. *(running out of bluff)* November's a particularly bad Isotta month. *(pause; nervous laugh; new brainwave; confidential)* Yeah, she's a

terror to work for — do this do that if my pants
aren't pressed just so she docks my pay. She says
I smell. She calls me a peasant. I'd quit, except
for the car. *(pause; he's gotten the OK)* Thank
you.

> *DANIEL returns to car. One frozen moment.*
> *They remain poker-faced as they drive forward.*
> *DANIEL's face is a study in absolute*
> *concentration as he shifts upward. As stage goes*
> *to black their faces split into wide grins of joy.*

9.

> *Music bridge. Venice. Night. HANNAH's*
> *palazzo. Lantern light, or flashlights.*
> *HANNAH is bringing DANIEL to his room.*

DANIEL Where's the light?

HANNAH There's no electricity on this floor.

DANIEL What kind of palace doesn't have electricity!

HANNAH This kind. My floor has it. Yours doesn't. I didn't
promise your father electricity. My stepmother's
family bought this old pile in the 20s — like
most of the grand houses, it was a wreck. We
only use it a few months each year; this floor is
superfluous. Washstands — towel. Vinetta says
the bed's fine and there's a view.

DANIEL I don't have a toothbrush.

HANNAH I'll send Vinetta up with one, and a razor. Do you
need a razor? I'm teasing Daniel. I'm sure you're
constantly shaving.

> *HANNAH is leaving.*

DANIEL Wait! Where are you going!

HANNAH I'm exhausted. I'll see you tomorrow.

DANIEL	Hannah?
HANNAH	You must be exhausted too.
DANIEL	No. I mean, yes I am. But what — what happens next?
HANNAH	I start making enquiries. About your passage. And I'll send a telegram to your father confirming our arrival. And then I am going to walk and walk and rejoice that I am back amongst civilized (people who)
DANIEL	I've always dreamt of Venice. I've been to Vienna and Salzburg of course but to see Venice, to see the (canals — Venice)
HANNAH	Uh — you aren't.
DANIEL	What?
HANNAH	This old house — for you, this is Venice. Last month things changed here, too. There are new laws — directed against refugees. That's you. You don't have papers, or a proper passport. Until I get a sense of the situation...
DANIEL	You should have told me this before!
HANNAH	Why. It's still safe here — but why take chances? It's for your own good. It won't be for long.

10.

A week later. A music bridge. Black, then lights up slowly on heavy breathing, sighing. DANIEL is under a blanket, masturbating. Just as lights come up, the door flies open and HANNAH barges in with tray. DANIEL furiously tries to cover himself with blanket or sheet.

HANNAH	Knock knock! Why! Still in bed, sleepyhead!

DANIEL	Nothing else to do.
HANNAH	Come now, covers off.

DANIEL hangs on to the sheet.

I'll buy you a radio today, will that help whatever ails you? *(tugs on sheet)* There is a library downstairs, you know.

DANIEL	It's all boring professor stuff.
HANNAH	Did you look on the top shelf, by the windows?
DANIEL	(Well no)
HANNAH	Because some of the books on that shelf have — photographs. *(tugs on sheet again)*
DANIEL	Stop it!
HANNAH	My my. Someone's getting up on the wrong side of the bed.
DANIEL	Where's Vinetta?
HANNAH	I gave her the day off. You've worn the poor thing out this past week, chasing her all over the house, practising your Italian on her, poor Vinetta with her terrible limp.
DANIEL	I'd like to get dressed...
HANNAH	You haven't heard my news! My uncle has *finally* agreed to see me, for dinner.
DANIEL	So?
HANNAH	So he's the one who'll arrange your passage.
DANIEL	Arrange it to where.

HANNAH   Anywhere that's not here. But it's not going to be
                as easy as I thought. Jews can't own businesses
                now, and we can't even have non-Jewish servants
                (and so)

DANIEL   But isn't Vinetta Catholic?

HANNAH   She needs the work. *(throughout following
                HANNAH will continually invade DANIEL's
                space, either by sitting too near him or
                "accidentally" pulling on the sheet)* So my uncle,
                he's preoccupied with selling his business, and
                arranging a passage might take a while. And he
                doesn't even like me — our families were
                estranged.

DANIEL   Why?

HANNAH   Uncle was a fascist. *(over DANIEL's groans.)* It
                wasn't uncommon here. It made sense, a lot of
                sense at the time.

DANIEL   For the capitalists.

HANNAH   *(nodding agreement)* He owns Venice's largest
                foundry. Mussolini appears, promising labour
                peace — Uncle takes the bait and a big family rift
                ensues. This is going to take every ounce of
                charm I possess.

DANIEL   I'm doomed.

                HANNAH laughs.

                Can I use your radio when you're gone?

HANNAH   It's by my bed. *(leaving)* Oh Daniel?

DANIEL   Yes?

HANNAH   As you were.

                *HANNAH laughs and leaves, pulling off the
                sheet as she goes.*

11.

That night, outside her room. HANNAH is changing, getting ready for bed. In some state of undress. Perhaps with her back to audience, combing out her hair. DANIEL is spying on her. HANNAH hears and stops combing, mid-stroke.

HANNAH

Is someone there? Daniel?

DANIEL knocks.

DANIEL

Do you want your radio back?

HANNAH

Keep it. The news is all depressing.

DANIEL

How did it — go with your uncle?

HANNAH

He gave me dinner. It wasn't so good; he's been forced to let his cook go. He's shipping out everything he owns in early January. It's going to take him all of December to get the permits. He thought he could arrange something for you on his boat.

DANIEL

Did you ask about my father?

HANNAH

He'll try to arrange a passport. But I'm afraid this all means you'll have to put up with me for another month. What's that you're holding?

DANIEL

I was showing Vinetta a few kitchen tricks. Kanzler's secret recipe. Mün cookies.

HANNAH

(takes one; starts to bite; stops) Anything else baked in here?

They laugh. HANNAH turns.

Your father taught you well. Could your brother make such good cookies?

DANIEL

No.

HANNAH   I didn't think so. He always struck me as more of
                  a bread man.

                  *HANNAH has let her top drop a bit, and combs
                  under her hair.*

                  Can you help me with something?

DANIEL   Help you?

HANNAH   The snap on this necklace.

DANIEL   I uh

HANNAH   It sticks

DANIEL   I don't think

HANNAH   It's so old. Can you feel it — tiny huh?

DANIEL   I'm not very good

HANNAH   Careful

DANIEL   I am being

HANNAH   Ow!

DANIEL   Sorry sorry. There. OK, got it.

                  *HANNAH turns, covering herself. She smiles
                  at DANIEL who is holding the necklace.*

HANNAH   You're the first man who ever got that off.

                  12.

                  *Christmas Eve, 1938. DANIEL's room. From
                  outside, the sound of church bells. HANNAH
                  bursts in with a book.*

HANNAH   I finally found it!

DANIEL	Don't you ever knock!
HANNAH	We're all friends here! Look! It wasn't on the top shelf after all; Father had locked it in his desk! He used to buy these in Paris. They cost a fortune. I liked these photographs — the Arab and his harem. And oh — look — palm trees!

DANIEL grabs the book and throws it.

DANIEL	I'm going crazy! I don't even have Vinetta to talk to.
HANNAH	It's Christmas Eve — she's gone to her family for a few days. I know this is boring for you — I'm sorry — but Vinetta's (had an idea)
DANIEL	You're sorry! That's a big help! You get to go out! You get to sit in cafes while I have to wait for your uncle. Five weeks in a drafty old pile — thank God one more week and I'm out of here.
HANNAH	(Actually)
DANIEL	At least on a boat I can walk the deck
HANNAH	(Daniel)
DANIEL	Stretch my legs, get some fresh air, more than the stink from that canal, is that water down there or just a toilet? Why is it so special to have a city built on open sewers? You're always raving about Venice, well all this place is, in my view, is a stinkhole, I'm counting (the days)
HANNAH	DANIEL! Don't you ever shut up! My uncle sent me a note. The boat — they loaded all the furniture on it — then the minute it was loaded the boat was embargoed.
DANIEL	What?

HANNAH   There's no boat. You can't leave! At least until
            we find something else. But dammit — what can
            that be, I mean, if my uncle's money is no use

            DANIEL is putting on a coat.

            What're you doing!

DANIEL   I'm going out!

HANNAH   Be patient! I'll find something.

DANIEL   When! In between gallery visits? When you've
            seen all the movies playing? *(leaving)*

HANNAH   *(grabs him)* WAIT!

DANIEL   "Wait"! That's all I ever hear!

HANNAH   There are still two months before all refugees have
            (to be out)

DANIEL   So they impound the boats just to make it a
            challenge? I've sat in here for four weeks, I don't
            care anymore, who cares if I don't have a passport.

HANNAH   I do! If they catch you they're going to ask you
            where you've been staying! Did you think of that?
            What will you say?

DANIEL   I'll invent something, like I did at the border.
            Don't worry Ma'am, you won't get in trouble.

            DANIEL rushes out. Black.

            13.

            *DANIEL is walking through Venice at night.
            Church bells are ringing in background.*

DANIEL   I am very alone. The mist, it should be
            comforting, it should make me feel secure, safe,
            but it only makes me lonely. Above me the bells

toll and around me the Christians keep appearing
and disappearing in the dark, filing to their
churches — and I am pulled along with them,
finding some comfort in that pious tide — I have
spent a month alone with no companion but
worry. We flow through the streets and alleys but
I step aside when we reach their churches. They
stop to make their sign and then look back at me.
Do they wonder why I edge back? I slip into the
mist and move on, looking for that place, a
refuge, a place where I can enter — a bakery or a
tailor's anywhere I don't care just anywhere I can
burst in and say, "I'm Daniel Kanzler I'm a Jew I
need help!" But there is no place marked "safe" and
there is no person I can ask — my Italian is too
bad and I look just a little bit different and I've
listened just a little too closely to the radio, to the
news of sporadic violence. I want to find the
ghetto, the Venetian ghetto, the first ghetto... But
I — But I can't find it and I can't find anything —
remotely welcoming — I am lost and that makes
me even lonelier, lonelier than I ever thought I
could be, and it makes me long for the palazzo,
for my prison — for Hannah.

14.

*Music bridge. Back at the Palazzo. DANIEL
enters and is met by HANNAH.*

HANNAH	Where did you go! *(no answer)* You idiot — where did you go!
DANIEL	I was sightseeing.
HANNAH	Were you in a bar?
DANIEL	Sure — hundreds of bars. I've been singing beer songs with the blackshirts.
HANNAH	This isn't a (joke)
DANIEL	I'm going up to my room.

HANNAH   What if someone had asked for your papers!

DANIEL   (Good night)

HANNAH   I was worried Daniel!

DANIEL   Oh were you.

                HANNAH kisses DANIEL long and hard.

HANNAH   Does that prove I was worried?

                *HANNAH kisses DANIEL again, and they ease
                on to the bed.*

HANNAH   My chauffeur used to say the Bugatti was like a
                woman — unpredictable and difficult to turn over.
                You learned to drive a Bugatti very quickly. Let's
                see how you are with a woman.

                *They resume kissing and then they begin
                making love. Light goes off them.*

                15.

                *Light comes up on to MISS PERRY. She is
                on the phone, conspiratorial.*

MISS PERRY   To keep it perfectly in period, to stick with the
                wartime motif, sir, I'm a Quisling, a Mata Hari, a
                Lord Haw-Haw. And I apologize for calling you at
                home like this Mr. Chairman Sir, but you simply
                must go to the Board of Directors. Call an
                emergency meeting! Why?! Because the owner and
                CEO of Mulgrave Corporation, Mr. Daniel
                McDougall Mulgrave is now convinced he's an
                Austrian Jew! He's digging canals in the parking
                lot! NO SIR, I HAVE NOT BEEN SMOKING
                MARY JANE! Oh sir, we are listing, this
                corporation is listing, have you seen our balance
                sheet lately? We're going down like the Titanic —
                no, make that the Athenia — yes, three
                smokestacks heading down, down to Davey Jones'

locker, oops just two stacks now, oops there goes another, and still there's a madman on deck, fiddling with his memories.

MULGRAVE appears beside MISS PERRY.

MULGRAVE   You're whispering on the phone again.

MISS PERRY   Boyfriend trouble, sorry.

MULGRAVE   I need you here, taking notes.

MISS PERRY   Mr. Mulgrave, sir.

MULGRAVE   Yes Miss Perry?

MISS PERRY   *Who* are Henry and Helga supposed to be playing? When we hired them you said Henry was you and Helga was your wife. You said she was your wife in Elora in a stone farmhouse and this all sounded plausible to me, but now, well, the tides of history seems to be washing in opposite directions. We seem to be Jewish now.

MULGRAVE   Yes.

MISS PERRY   And popping Venetian cherries.

MULGRAVE   I know.

MISS PERRY   So this is all true? That's really you?

MULGRAVE   I'm afraid so. I really hadn't intended any of this. I thought the Elora story would solve everything, thought they would give my memoirs just the right Horatio Alger-type accent. It didn't work.

MISS PERRY   Then if he's you, who in God's name is she?

MULGRAVE   In due course, Miss Perry. Look!

MISS PERRY and MULGRAVE raise their binoculars and watch HANNAH and DANIEL for a moment.

MULGRAVE   Ah, I pity the youth of today, Miss Perry, all that
                  casual discotheque business, the cheap, easy
                  liaisons, the speed at which they toss off their
                  virginity. None of them will possess a memory
                  like mine. Were you ever a virgin, Miss Perry?

MISS PERRY   No sir. Never.

MULGRAVE   I'm sorry.

MISS PERRY   I thought once I might be — a virgin — but it
                  turned out to be gas.

MULGRAVE   The most important part of the story is
                  beginning. Here's their next scene. Take it to
                  them.

MISS PERRY   Now?

MULGRAVE   Now.

MISS PERRY   They're a bit — busy.

MULGRAVE   They'll be done by the time you get there.
                  Vinetta.

MISS PERRY   "Vinetta" sir?

MULGRAVE   She was very shy, unworldly. A good, devout
                  Catholic with a terrible limp, who treated me with
                  dignity. OK. Off with you now.

                  MISS PERRY limps out.

                  I didn't pause to question Hannah's motives —
                  pity, attraction, perhaps just relief that I hadn't
                  been harmed in my ramble outside. I only knew
                  that in my eighteen years of sameness, in my
                  eighteen years of growing up in exactly the same
                  place with exactly the same people I had never
                  met anyone like her. I had only known my father,
                  and my brother, and a finite variety of bread,
                  pastry, and customers. And girls. The same girls.
                  The same not-having of girls. The endless seeing

but not-touching of girls; gentile girls, field girls,
town girls and the innaccessible trio of Jewish
girls my age: rich Sarah Sarah what was her — ah
Sarah Goldschmidt with her long thin legs that
she wrapped around — horses only; Rosa —
Strauss, gentle Rosa who came every day to the
shop with her mother to eat pastries until they
both had matching sugar mustaches; and finally
Eva Mayer, Eva of a thousand dreams, Eva
swinging down our alley to our shop, scorching
the stone walls with her hips, oblivious to me,
turning my brother to stuttering rubber. That was
all I knew, until her. Where is she?!

16.

*Back at the farmhouse now. HANNAH and
DANIEL — now reverted to HENRY and
HELGA — are relaxing after the sex.*

HANNAH   That was brilliant.

DANIEL   You don't think I was too — I don't know —
unvirginal?

HANNAH   Mulgrave probably can't tell from up there.

DANIEL   It's tough, acting like we've never done it before.
But hey — did you notice how I went lickety-split
like a guy's first time?

HANNAH   Oh, I thought you were just being yourself!
(pause) Yes, Henry, I noticed.

DANIEL   I even visualized our great Prime Ministers, in
reverse order, like when we started. To slow me
down.

HANNAH   So that's why every time you came you'd yell
"Diefenbaker"!

They laugh.

DANIEL   We really are insane.

HANNAH   What about Mulgrave! And that disco dinosaur.

> *MISS PERRY is appearing behind their bed.*
> *She has brought the priest's robes with her.*

DANIEL   Old Miss Quasimodo. Do you think she and
Mulgrave are an item?

HANNAH   In her dreams.

MISS PERRY   Madame Hannah excuse me for interrupting but I
have brought the gift I promised — a present from
Father — uh Mulgravio. And from old Vinetta,
too. With love. Because your young gentleman
caller really must get out and stretch his legs. The
other two. *(hands package over)* I had the devil of
the time getting here. My vaporetto she sprang a
leak on The Grand Canal, and sank. I had to hitch
a ride on a gondola. With a gaggle of Gregorian
monks. Funny guys those Gregorians! Always
chanting, one note only! "Satan he twitches 'neath
my robes." Now I'll leave you lovebirds.
Vinetta's got mass. Ciao. Ciao.

> *MISS PERRY is exiting.*

HANNAH   Your limp!

> *MISS PERRY swears in Italian, and exits,*
> *limping. DANIEL picks up the package; he and*
> *HANNAH are back in character.*

DANIEL   What's this?

HANNAH   Go ahead — try it on — it should fit better than
the chauffeur's uniform.

DANIEL   *(dressing in priest's outfit)* But why?

HANNAH	I thought it would be a wonderful way to see the city — a young woman in the company of a priest, her brother, perhaps home for a Christmas visit. What could be more above reproach?
DANIEL	What if someone comes up to me — what if they ask me something? Something Christian? Catholics make that weird sign. *(tries crossing himself, gets it wrong)*
HANNAH	I don't think that's it.
DANIEL	They're always doing it. Like a nervous tic. *(tries again, does it wrong)*
HANNAH	Vinetta can give you a lesson.
	HANNAH begins kissing him again.
DANIEL	Suddenly this doesn't feel proper.
HANNAH	When it feels proper, it's time to quit.

17.

Full light. Venice. Two weeks into January, 1939. Piazza San Marco. DANIEL and HANNAH are standing with their backs to the audience. DANIEL is dressed as a priest. He is copping a feel. HANNAH pushes his hand away.

HANNAH	That, of course, is the doge's palace.
DANIEL	*(repeating, with fun)* The doge. Doge.
HANNAH	You shouldn't touch me there, not here. Don't!
DANIEL	I don't care.

HANNAH	I do! You can hold my arm. The elbow. Now, can you see the mishmash of Byzantine, Gothic and Renaissance styling in the Basilica? You know I don't know why we didn't come out here sooner! It's really fun being a tour guide — this is the greatest city on earth and look!

DANIEL raises binoculars, looks up with them, then trains them back down on HANNAH's breasts as she talks.

See those horses — they're bronze — they were stolen from Constantinople when Venice attacked it in the 4th Crusade, 1204. Don't do that. If you don't behave you (can't come out!)

DANIEL	Let's go back in.
HANNAH	You spent all of December begging me to go out, now we're out ten minutes and you want to go back in! Why!
DANIEL	Doge.
HANNAH	All right. We'll go back. But first you have to see the Bridge of Sighs. I think of all the bridges in Venice it's my favourite. The condemned would walk it after sentencing — from the courthouse to the jail — or execution. Hence the sighs. It's just around the corner.

DANIEL is touching her.

Don't — someone's coming.

Someone passes by. Sees DANIEL and crosses himself.

DANIEL	He did the sign to me!

DANIEL crosses himself back, ostentatiously, and smiles broadly at the passerby.

There's another one!

DANIEL crosses himself again.

HANNAH   Don't cross back! It's not a salute!

DANIEL   They thought I was a priest!

HANNAH   Thank God they did. Now come and see the bridge. Oh Daniel, this is why I came to Europe. You have no idea what I left behind — your bakery was easy street compared to how I lived in Toronto. Look at this! *(pause)* But funny, I've been here a dozen times before and it's never been this beautiful — why is that?

DANIEL   Doge?

HANNAH   Just doge?

DANIEL   No. More than that.

The Bridge of Sighs appears behind them; there is a swastika on it. They turn and see it. Black.

18.

Music bridge. HANNAH and DANIEL are coming home from seeing the bridge. They meet MULGRAVE and he hands a letter to HANNAH.

HANNAH   It's for you.

DANIEL   Father? *(taking it)* No, it's not his handwriting.

DANIEL is ripping letter open.

This doesn't look good, it's our neighbours, they say they *(reading)*

HANNAH   (What)

DANIEL   *(hands letter over)* Our shop was torched. He was arrested.

HANNAH comes to him.

DANIEL	They don't know where he is.
HANNAH	But he knows where you are. When they release (him he can)
DANIEL	They're not releasing him. They haven't let my brother go, or your father, they aren't releasing anyone. I want to go to Palestine, now!
HANNAH	Calm down! Be reasonable!
DANIEL	I promised him!
HANNAH	You're safe here!
DANIEL	We are not safe!
HANNAH	No one knows you're here!
DANIEL	Vinetta knows! Her priest knows!
HANNAH	They're completely trustworthy!
DANIEL	Someone else might have seen us! We've got to go now!
HANNAH	There are no ships!
DANIEL	You stopped trying!
HANNAH	We can stay here! Daniel — this is not Germany, it's not Austria, it's Italy, it's not the same, stay here, stay with me, we can wait this thing out!
DANIEL	*(calm now)* You saved me in Austria — I didn't know it was time to go but you did. Now — I know it is time to leave here, trust me, trust me, every instinct says, let's go now.
HANNAH	I'm going to wait until my father comes.
DANIEL	He's not coming!

HANNAH slaps him.

HANNAH   He'll be here.

19.

Not much later. Late January 1939. Harbour, shipyard sounds. Light up on DANIEL, in priest's outfit.

DANIEL   I need a passage to — Palestine. The Holy Land. This month. Why does it have to be February? It's — a promise. I made. To God. And to the Pope. Pius the Eleventh. Twelfth. All the berths are taken? Is that a definite no? You do see that I'm a *(indicating he's a priest)*. I don't know who else you've booked on that boat, but I would suggest strongly to you, my friend, that you give priority to — well yes I look young for a priest, everyone says that — the Cardinal said that, and I am young, it's true, I'm somewhat of a — prodigy. Would this help you to make up your mind?

DANIEL pulls necklace from pocket. He hands it to MULGRAVE.

20.

MULGRAVE takes the necklace. He turns to MISS PERRY.

MULGRAVE   He took the necklace and I got my ticket. He got a necklace. I got my freedom.

MISS PERRY   Sir. Working for you has been the greatest — and only — honour of my pathetic life.

MULGRAVE   Why thank you Miss Perry.

MISS PERRY	I'm not done. Sir, it is with great heaviness of heart that I must tell you that your Board of Directors is meeting downstairs, right now.
MULGRAVE	Oh? That's nice. *(resumes watching)*
MISS PERRY	No, it's not nice at all. After that meeting — which will be short because the evidence against your sanity is so compelling — the Board Chairman will call me, and request an appointment with you. I will usher him in here and together you will look down over your parking lot with that stone farmhouse and your Bugatti, and my ancient bicycle, and the Venetian canals you've dug. He will look down with you, perhaps he'll put his arm on your shoulder; what is certain is that he will tell you: it is time for you to go.
MULGRAVE	I am prepared for that. Thank you — Miss Perry.
MISS PERRY	*(touches his cheek)* Will that be all then, sir?
MULGRAVE	Yes, thank you. You may go and call the Chairman.

MISS PERRY exits. MULGRAVE turns to watch the following:

21.

Music. Light up on HANNAH's bed. DANIEL is getting out of it, in moonlight, and dresses quickly in the priest's outfit. Once dressed he pulls a small suitcase or bag from under the bed and begins to creep out of the room. He pauses, then returns, kisses the sleeping HANNAH, who stirs.

HANNAH	Daniel. Daniel? Why are you dressed?
DANIEL	I'm leaving.

HANNAH	What!
DANIEL	There's a boat leaving, at dawn.
HANNAH	NO!

HANNAH tries to pull him down on the bed. DANIEL struggles to extricate himself.

DANIEL	I asked you to come (I begged you I told you I was going)
HANNAH	I will (I will come I promise I'll come)
DANIEL	I've bought my passage. *(goes for door, stops, turns)* I love you Hannah, but it's too late. I'll send you my address. When you are ready to leave...

DANIEL turns to leave — he is in the listening pose.

HANNAH	Wait! Daniel! DANIEL! I'm pregnant.

DANIEL hears this, but keeps going, moving to the second half of his pose. Just before the stage goes black he is frozen in his leave-taking pose, the same pose that started both "The Man Without Memories" and "The Bridge of Sighs".

22.

MULGRAVE is alone.

MULGRAVE	I didn't write. I suppose I could rationalize by saying a letter to her — from Palestine — might have drawn unwelcome attention from the authorities. And I don't know what became of her. I never went back. Hannah. Hannah. What became of you?

Light back up on HANNAH. She is at the same stage of pregnancy as was HELGA in "The Man Without Memories". She is finishing a letter.

HANNAH   Mother. Please read this. I am in Venice, at father's palazzo. Actually, the word is too grand; it might as well be a prison, because I can't leave it. I'm going to have a child and the pregnancy is difficult. The father is in Palestine; I did not marry him because — *(idea)* because I will not be shackled by such bourgeois conventions. That should make you proud. Mother, I will start writing to you every week, and I will send money. If you stop hearing from me, you must come to Venice (and take this baby home)

MOTHER   *(voice over only, coming in over HANNAH)* take this baby home with you and raise her in Canada. Yes, I'm sure it will be a girl. A granddaughter for you. She will be in the care of my maid, Vinetta, and you can ask for her at the address below.

Black on MOTHER. Full light on MULGRAVE.

MULGRAVE   I will never know.

MULGRAVE trains his binoculars on HANNAH. She is no longer pregnant. Her back is to the audience. There are sounds of doors pounded, curses. HANNAH turns. She stands there with her suitcase and then walks forward a few steps. Light down on HANNAH and up on MOTHER, who is much older, perhaps with glasses, but still sitting with her feet in the tub, speaking now to her granddaughter, BETTY.

MOTHER   Who would have thought I should live through two wars and still be working like a dog? I started when I was nine, gluing paper bags. At fourteen I was apprenticed to a wigmaker — did I tell you that? Betty! Where is the water for my feet? Your fancy friends might have a television and listen to that awful music, but I am still your grandmother and you must obey me for a few years yet.

BETTY appears as a 15-year old, with water basin.

Now tonight we'll stay up late; I feel like talking. I can tell you some stories that are better than anything on your friends' television sets. *(gentle)* Betty? Come here. Come my little flower.

BETTY and MOTHER hug.

MULGRAVE   *(putting down binoculars)* No, I will never know. And if you can never know, you can't have the memory. And if you can't ever remember, you can't ever be hurt. Can you.

Light back up on HANNAH. She is standing there, with clear sound of train and symphony. HANNAH takes a few steps backwards, just as she did at the end of "My Mother's Luck".

Black.

The End.

Other plays by Dave Carley...

Taking Liberties & Into
ISBN 0-88754-512-2 / $10.95
Playwrights Canada Press

"Hedges" in *Six Canadian Plays*
ISBN 0-88754-469-X / $14.95
Playwrights Canada Press

After You
ISBN 1-896239-00-5 / $12.95
Scirocco Drama

Midnight Madness
ISBN 0-920197-88-4 / $9.95
Blizzard Publishing

Writing With Our Feet
ISBN 0-921368-20-8 / $10.98
Blizzard Publishing